English Code 5

Phonics Book

International Phonetic Alphabet (IPA)

Consonants

/b/	bag, bike
/d/	desk, opened
/f/	face, free, laugh, photo
/g/	game, good
/h/	hit, hot
/k/	key, kite
/l/	lamp, lucky
/m/	man, monkey
/n/	neck, nut
/ŋ/	ring, flying
/p/	pen, pink
/r/	run, rock
/s/	sun, sell, cycle, grapes
/ʃ/	shirt, shut, shell
/t/	tent, knocked
/θ/	thick, thirsty
/ð/	this, there
/v/	visit, give
/w/	wall, window, what
/ks/	relax, taxi
/j/	yellow, young
/z/	zoo, bananas
/tʃ/	chair, cheese, cheap
/dʒ/	jeans, juice, judge, ginger

Two-Letter Consonant Blend

/bl/	blanket, blue
/pl/	plane, planet
/kl/	clean, climb
/gl/	glass, glove
/fl/	fly, floor
/sl/	sleep, slow
/br/	break, branch
/pr/	price, practice
/kr/	crab
/fr/	fruit
/gr/	grass
/dr/	draw
/tr/	train
/ŋk/	bank, think
/nd/	stand, round
/nt/	student, count
/sk/	scarf, skirt, basket, scary
/sm/	small
/sn/	snow
/sp/	sports, space
/st/	stand, first, stay
/sw/	swim, sweet
/tw/	twelve, twins
/kw/	quick, question

Three-Letter Consonant Blend

/spr/	spring
/str/	street
/skr/	screen
/skw/	square

Vowels

🇺🇸 /ɑː/ 🇬🇧 /ɒ/	top, jog, wash
/æ/	cat, clap, sand
/e/	wet, send, healthy
/ɪ/	hit, sing, pin
/ɔː/	caught, saw, cough
🇺🇸 /ɔːr/ 🇬🇧 /ɔː/	horse, morning
/eɪ/	cake, name, say
/iː/	eat, tree, steam
🇺🇸 /oʊ/ 🇬🇧 /əʊ/	home, coat, snow
/uː/	food, glue, flew, June
/ʌ/	duck, run, cut, honey
/ʊ/	cook, foot, put
🇺🇸 /ər/ 🇬🇧 /ə/	ruler, teacher
/ɜːr/	bird, hurt, word, learn

Diphthongs

/aɪ/	nice, bike
/aʊ/	house, brown
/ɔɪ/	boil, enjoy
🇺🇸 /aːr/ 🇬🇧 /aː/	card, market
🇺🇸 /aɪr/ 🇬🇧 /aɪə/	fire, hire
🇺🇸 /aʊr/, /aʊər/ 🇬🇧 /aʊər/	hour, flower
🇺🇸 /er/ 🇬🇧 /eə/	chair, bear, there
🇺🇸 /ɪr/ 🇬🇧 /ɪə/	near, engineer
/juː/	cute, huge, few

Vowel and Consonant Blend

/ʃən/	station, dictionary
/ɪz/	beaches, bridges
/ɪd/	visited

Contents

1   nk

1   Listen, point, and repeat.

1

ba**nk**

2

dri**nk**

3
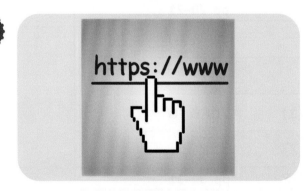
li**nk**

4
li**nk**

pi**nk**

5

thi**nk**

6

tru**nk**

2  Listen. Then say.

I like to think of a pink pineapple drink.

A cherry on the top would slowly sink

in the pink pineapple drink.

3 Design another drink. Make a new tongue twister with a partner.

1 ng

1
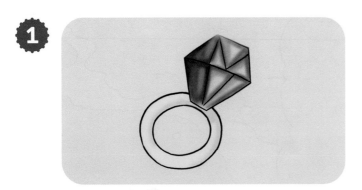
ring

2

swing

3

king

4

sing

5

flying

6

trying

5 🎵 Listen. Then sing.

I want to sing,
Sing a song
Fit for a king.
I want to bring
A little happiness in a song.
I want to sing,
Sing a song
Fit for a king.

6 **What do the other birds want to do? Write a chant beginning with *I want to ... .* Then tell a partner.**

2

nt

1 🎧 07 Listen, point, and repeat.

1

ant

2

count

3

plant

4
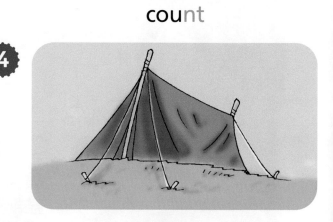
tent

5

student

6

accident

2 🎧 💬 Listen and read.

1 A little ant lives with his family under a plant.

2 On Sunday, they went to visit their aunt.

3 She lives in a tiny tent.

4 They all went in and had an ant party!

3 💡 💬 What did the ants eat at their party? Tell a partner.

2 nd

4 Listen, point, and repeat.

1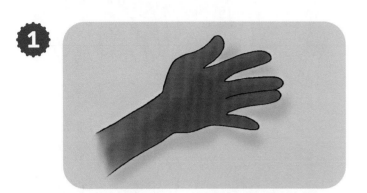

hand

2

lend

3

pond

4

around

5

stand

6

behind

5 Listen and read.

1

Let's go fishing on Saturday.

Where shall we meet?

2

If you stand behind the pond, I'll come around the corner.

3

I'll put my hand in the air and wave.

4

I can lend you my brother's fishing rod.

6 Tell your classmates to stand in different places in the classroom.

Stand near the door!

Review 1

1 🎧11 💬 Listen and say the words.

1. win — wing

2. sick — sink

3. sad — sand

4. hut — hunt

2 **Now listen and write the words.**

_____ n	_____ ng
_____	_____
_____	_____
_____ ck	_____ nk
_____	_____
_____	_____
_____ d	_____ nd
_____	_____
_____	_____
_____ t	_____ nt
_____	_____
_____	_____

3

st

1 Listen, point, and repeat.

1

best

2
fast

3
first

4
artist

5
August

6
dentist

2 🎧 💬 Listen and read.

1 It's wonderful to be an artist.

2 First, you find something to paint. Then find the best place to stand.

3 You can paint fast or slowly.

4 Painting in August is the best!

3 💡 💬 Why is painting in August the best? Tell a partner.

3

sk

4 🎧 15 **Listen, point, and repeat.**

1

a**sk**

2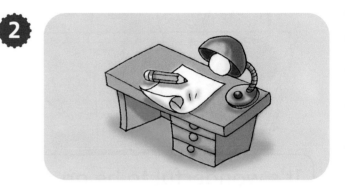

de**sk**

3

ba**sk**et

4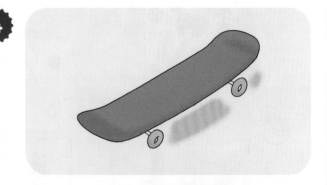

skateboard

5

ma**sk**

6

whi**sk**

5 🔧 💬 Listen and read.

Never a**sk** somebody wearing a ma**sk**
to do a difficult ta**sk**.
Never a**sk** somebody on a **sk**ateboard
to whi**sk** an egg in a ba**sk**et.

6 💡 What other sports does the boy do?

4 gh / ph

1 **Listen, point, and repeat.**

gh

ph

1

cough

2

phone

3

laugh

4

photo

5

rough

6

elephant

It's tough to phone an elephant.

He never answers the phone!

All you can hear is the elephant laugh.

Why not try to phone a giraffe?

3 **Work in pairs. Role-play a telephone conversation with the elephant or the giraffe.**

4 tion

4 🎧 19 Listen, point, and repeat.

1

station

2

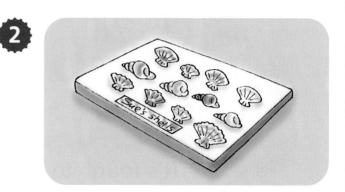

collection

3

invention

4

dictionary

5

information

6

invitation

5 🎵 Listen. Then sing.

Asking for explanations
Can make you very wise.
Collecting information
Can be a big surprise.
If you use your imagination,
The next invention
Could win you a very special prize.

6 **Where can you find different kinds of information? Tell a partner.**

Review 2

st

sk

1 🗨 Play the game. Say words with the letters in the squares.

tion **4**

ph **5**

gh **6**

sk **7**

st **3**

st **2**

tion **8**

sk **1**

ph **9**

10 s

GO!

20

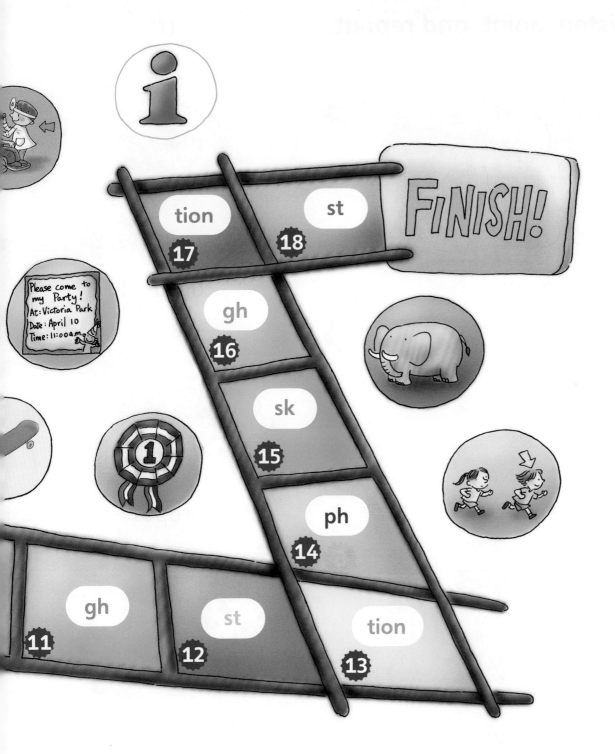

5

Plural (1)

1 Listen, point, and repeat.

1

pears

2

lemons

3

bananas

4

cupcakes

5
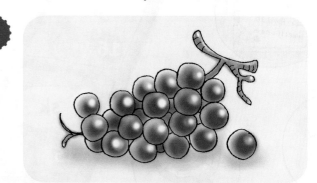
grapes

6
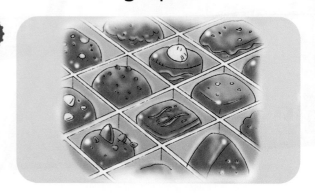
chocolates

2  **Listen. Then say.**

Melons and grapefruits,
Strawberries and cream.
Bananas and mangoes,
What a great dream!
Lemons and pears,
Apples and grapes.
Cherries and chocolates,
All kinds of ice cream!

Cats and
dogs …

3 **Write a chant about animals.
Then tell a partner.**

Plural (2)

 Listen, point, and repeat.

1

beach**es**

2

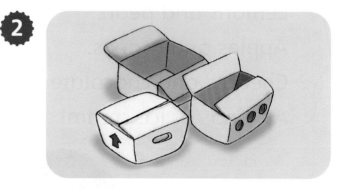

box**es**

3

bus**es**

4

dish**es**

5

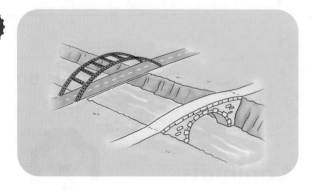

bridge**s**

6

prize**s**

5 🎧 💬 **Listen. Then say.**

In summer we pack our suitcases,
make sandwiches for our lunches,
and go on buses to the beaches.

6 ⚙️ **Write a short dialog between the children.**
Act it out with a partner.

6 Past Tense (1)

1 Listen, point, and repeat.

1

cleaned

2

opened

3

arrived

4

searched

5

knocked

6

laughed

 **Listen and read.**

Did you do anything exciting last weekend?

I was unhappy because I was alone, so I asked Dad if some friends could come and play.

When they arrived, they knocked on our door. Dad opened the door and eleven children walked in!

We had a great day!

3 **What did you do last weekend? Tell the class.**

4 Listen, point, and repeat.

1

acted

2

added

3

handed

4

mended

5

rested

6

visited

5 🔧 💬 Listen. Then say.

I knocked on your door,
You hand**ed** me a phone,
We telephon**ed** our friends
To see if they were home.

We want**ed** to go shopping,
Then we visit**ed** the park.
We rent**ed** a computer game
And walked home in the dark.

6 💬 Did you do anything special with your friends last week? Tell a partner.

Review 3

Plural (1)

1 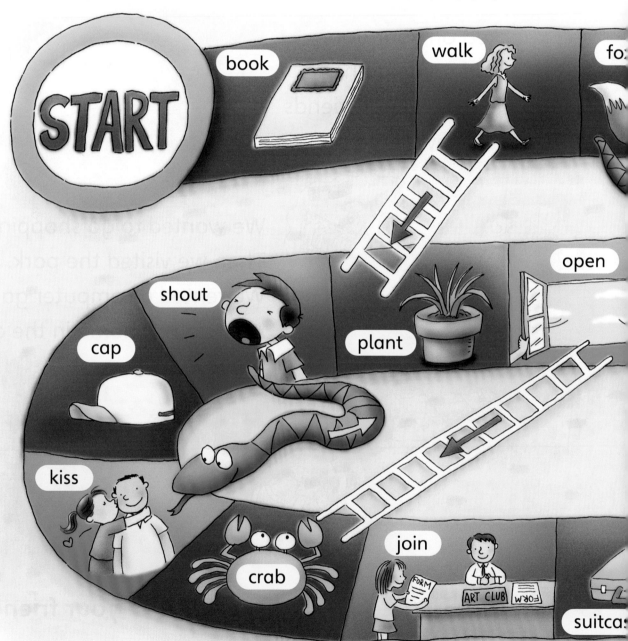 Play the game. On a red square, say the plural of the word. On a blue square, say the Past Tense of the word. Then listen and check.

book

walk

fox

START

open

shout

plant

cap

kiss

crab

join

suitcase

listen

brush

visit

bed

dog

glass

lunch

banana

FINISH

7

1 🎧 31 Listen, point, and repeat.

sp

1

space

2

spices

3

special

spr

4

spray

5

spring

6

spread

2 🔊 💬 Listen and read.

It's spring.
The baby birds are learning to fly.
They spread their wings and take off.
They glide through the air.
There's so much space in the sky.
It's a special time!

3 💡 💬 What do you like doing in spring? Tell a partner.

7

4 Listen, point, and repeat.

 st

 str

 1

st**ain**

 4

str**anger**

 2

st**ay**

5

str**ay**

 3

st**eep**

6

str**eet**

5 🔊 34 💬 **Listen. Then say.**

If you stray too far
On a very steep street,
Don't talk to strangers
Or stay very long.
Walk back down the steep street
And stay where you belong.

6 ⚙️ 💬 **Draw the street where you live.
Then tell the class.**

8

sc / **sk** **scr**

1 🎧 35 Listen, point, and repeat.

 sc / **sk**   **scr**

1

scary

2

skin

3

scanner

4

scream

5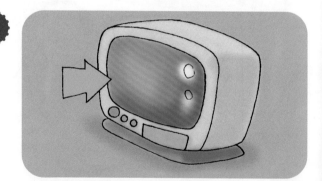

screen

6

scrapbook

2 Listen. Then say.

There's a scary movie
On the TV screen.
You can hear creepy music
And the sound of a scream.
I'd prefer to read a scrapbook
Or a nice magazine!

3 Draw a word that begins with *scr* and show it to the class.

8

 sc / sk squ

 4 Listen, point, and repeat.

sc / sk squ

1

sky

4
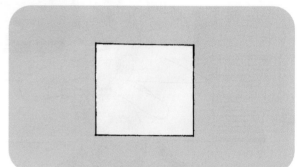
square

2

Scot

5

squash

3
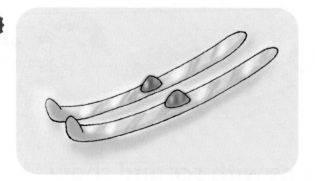
skis

6

squeeze

5 🎧 💬 Listen. Then say.

Can you squeeze a lemon?
Can you squash a plum?
Can you draw a square
On your finger or your thumb?
You can never scare a Scot
By banging on a drum!

6 ⚙️ Write down five things that have a square shape. Then compare with a partner.

Review 4

sp
spr

1 🎧 39 Listen and say the words.

1

spin   **spr**ing

2

steep   **str**eet

3

scare   **squ**are

4

space   **spr**ay

5

sky   **scr**eam

6

skis   **squ**eeze

7

stay   **str**ay

8

scanner   **scr**apbook

9

screen   **squ**eeze

st
str

sc / sk

scr

squ

2 💬 **Choose and write nine words. Play *Bingo*.**

1	**2**	**3**
4	**5**	**6**
7	**8**	**9**

PHONICS DICTIONARY

 nk

bank	drink	link	pink	think	trunk

 ng

ring	swing	king	sing	flying	trying

 nt

ant	count	plant	tent	student	accident

 nd

hand	lend	pond	around	stand	behind

st best fast first artist August dentist

sk ask desk basket skateboard mask whisk

gh
ph cough laugh rough phone photo elephant

tion station collection invention dictionary

information invitation

PHONICS DICTIONARY

Plural (1)

pears   lemons   bananas   cupcakes   grapes   chocolates

Plural (2)

beaches   boxes   buses   dishes   bridges   prizes

Past Tense (1)

cleaned   opened   arrived   searched   knocked   laughed

Past Tense (2)

acted   added   handed   mended   rested   visited

| **sp** / **sp** | space | spices | special | spray | spring | spread |

| **st** / **str** | stain | stay | steep | stranger | stray | street |

| **sc/sk** / **scr** | scary | skin | scanner | scream | screen | scrapbook |

| **sc/sk** / **squ** | sky | Scot | skis | square | squash | squeeze |

Pearson Education Limited
KAO TWO
KAO Park
Hockham Way
Harlow, Essex
CM17 9SR
England
and Associated Companies throughout the world.

english.com/englishcode

Authorized Licenced Edition from the English language edition, entitled Phonics Fun, 1st edition
published Pearson Education Asia Limited, Hong Kong and Longman Asia ELT © 2003.

This Edition © Pearson Education Limited 2021

First published 2021
Fourth impression 2024
ISBN: 978-1-292-32263-6
Set in Heinemann Roman 17/19pt
Printed in Slovakia by Neografia
Illustrated by Christos Skaltsas (Hyphen S.A.)